TIERS OF HEALING IV

Self Guided Workbook...Journey To a New Reality

by

ANNE BROWNING

TIERS OF HEALING
OVERVIEW AND WELCOME

Welcome to Tiers of Healing. We have been where you are. Each of us has suffered great loss; we have grieved, and we too have had thoughts that life would never be good again.

We want to encourage you that life will be good again.

If we were able to move from a place of hopelessness and despair to a place where there was a glimmer of hope, we know you will be able to do the same. If we were able to build on that hope and find a grudging sense of acceptance for all that was lost to us, we know that you will be able to do the same. If each of us was able to find a new vision for what would become our new normal, we are certain it is possible for you.

Finally, if we, with little support, were able to take the steps to reach that vision and live a full and joyful life, we know you will have the ability to take those steps. We are here to support you.

Tiers of Healing was originally designed to be facilitated in small groups. That product is still available, and there are groups that meet to move through all the tiers of loss, their members finding hope and friendship along the way.

This book has many of the components of our group program, but it is designed for individual study. We urge you to find someone to share your journey with, perhaps a trusted friend, mentor, or coach. We welcome your sharing through anne@tiersofhealing.com.

To make the most of this material, allow yourself the gift of time. Healing from loss is possible if you decide to do the work that is required. The amount of time will vary with each individual, but a maximum of three hours per day and a minimum of forty minutes is a good place to begin. Know that you are not alone.

The exercises in these workbooks are not difficult, yet they can be profound. Because of this, each lesson must be assimilated before moving forward to the next.

Find a quiet place and consecrate it for your healing. Bless the space, perhaps adding flowers or meaningful mementos. You will need a place to write and some writing materials. Some of the exercises in this book ask you to have crayons or even modeling clay. Please note supplies needed at the start of each session.

A session takes approximately ten to fifteen minutes to read (some might take longer). You will need an additional fifteen to thirty minutes for the exercises.

We have included an emotional Weather Report Chart. This is an important tool, and we urge you to copy it and keep it in a place where you can make notes on it daily. Very often during times of loss and chaos, we feel as if we are not making progress. The Weather Report is an excellent tool to note those days that were happy/sunny, and to aid you in noting what it was you did or what you were thinking that helped make the day sunny. Equally, it can be a great way to note if you are in a place where day after day, week after week you appear to be getting worse. We urge each of you to care for yourself and to seek professional help for working through your grief in addition to using this self-help guide. It may take a village to raise a child, but it takes an army to heal the loss of one.

We celebrate your courage. Loss must be healed. It has a way of hiding deep within the soul robbing us of energy, joy, and motivation. We believe we have "gotten past it," yet as we view the world, we are easily angered, we tire more quickly, or we just see the world as a place of dreary sameness. When the hurt has healed, the joy in living returns and life becomes hopeful once again.

At no time do we tell you that it is not painful. It is. At no time do we tell you that you will stop the missing. You won't. At no time do we tell you that life will be as it used to be. It will not. What we *will* tell you is that pain comes to us all, but misery is a choice, and you can choose to move out of it. What we will tell you is that there is always something to miss as you grow, yet there can be smiles and laughter and joyful memories, not longing.

Finally, we will tell you that you do not know what is up ahead. Life has changed; there will be more joys, more laughter, and more love. It will be different than it was; it will be your new normal, and you may like it. There is at least hope that you will one day be on the other side of your loss, and you will be okay. We know; we have travelled the path, and we are okay. Most days we are better than okay.

Again, welcome to Tiers of Healing. We are here for you and with you.

Contact info:

anne@tiersofhealing.com

ACKNOWLEDGMENTS

Tiers of Healing Self Study Guides are based on a program Linda Debelser Owen and I created. The four-part program is designed for small groups. Tiers of Healing for groups, was and continues to be, a mission of love for both Linda and myself. I owe a deep thanks to Linda for her vision, her dedication, and most importantly, her friendship.

There were months and months of talks, writing, rewriting, editing and more editing and rewriting. Not once did I hear Linda complain about the work involved. She kept her eye on her vision of reaching hurting people and helping them heal. Linda lives in Canada and runs the Canadian Tiers program. She has delivered the group material to churches, women fighting breast cancer, indigenous people who are still recovering from land loss and she is the woman I turn to when I need a laugh, a push or a strong shoulder. She is my hero. I acknowledge her expertise, her commitment, her integrity and her love.

I want to acknowledge all the men, women and children who have had a loss and continue to live their lives fully and who have the compassion to reach out to others who are in pain. I acknowledge those to whom this book is dedicated, individuals who are in pain and feel alone. I assure you, you are *not* alone.

We are here and we have known your pain.

Donna Lipman of Austin Texas is the woman who recorded the DVD portion of the Tiers of Healing for Groups. She is a woman of deep compassion, brilliant insights. Her commitment to filling our world with peace and joy was begun at birth. Everyone adores Donna. She has delivered the Tiers for Groups in Austin and she used the material in a very real way when her husband, Terry Lipman, who did the filming for the DVD, died suddenly. I acknowledge her, love her and treasure her friendship.

My husband, Peter Schroeder, helped Linda and I with the editing and reading of Tiers of Healing for Groups. He was instrumental in getting the Tiers of Healing Self Study Guides completed and is editing Tiers of Helping and Tiers of Hope. Peter is the miracle that God sent to me as answered prayer in 1988. He continues to inspire me, strengthen me, hold me and without him my life would be much less bright. I love you, Peter.

Finally, I must acknowledge my mentor, teacher and friend, Debbie Ford. Thank you, Debbie for your work, your guidance, your love.

TIERS OF HEALING
TIER IV JOURNEY TO A NEW REALITY
SELF-GUIDED WORKBOOK IV

TIERS OF HEALING IV
SESSION 1
SELF-CARE REVIEW

Acceptance of ourselves is the beginning of personal growth and transformation. In accepting ourselves, we face the fact of our own fragility and incompleteness, and it is by acknowledging that we are incomplete that we can change. Peace of mind is achieved not by filling in the gaps or correcting the flaws in our personality, but in understanding these flaws and accepting them as part of our reality.
From *Gardening the Soul by Sister* Stanislaus Kennedy

Song: "Welcome to Wherever You Are" by Jon Bon Jovi

In Tier III, we talked about visioning and the power of your directed thoughts. You created a powerful vision that will draw you forward, just as the beacon of light from a lighthouse draws ships over the rough seas and toward the shore. In Tier III, you set personal goals and learned additional ways to celebrate yourself and your life. You began to take the steps that would move you to the next Tier in your journey of healing, your New Reality.

As we begin The Journey to a New Reality for our lives, it is important for us to acknowledge where we are now. We ended Tier III by embracing the need for play, laughter, and fun in our lives.

Please be certain you continue with this important task. You may want to add to your Self-Care Contract a time to play, have fun, or just to laugh.

Please continue tracking your moods and emotions. Remember, you may compare these emotions to the weather (sad=rainy; happy=sunny; angry=stormy). What is important is that you keep a record of your progress. Sometimes the work of healing from loss can seem overwhelming, and it is easy to lose track of the strides you make unless you keep a record of your emotional growth.

Remember that it is your responsibility to put yourself first, to love yourself unconditionally, and to nurture yourself when you need nurturing. It is your responsibility to honor yourself and to schedule time to laugh and play and to have fun. When you are able to take care of yourself first, you then become able to take care of others.

At the end of Tier I, we asked you to get an acknowledgment box, and at the end of Tier II, we asked that you continue to use it as you practiced honoring yourself at the deepest level. In Tier IV, we ask you to continue both practices, as you add new ones.

We have also talked about gratitude. We had you make a list of all the things to be grateful for in the various areas of your life. We urge you to continue setting aside time to find reasons for gratitude in your life. Gratitude is your doorway to joy.

In Tier III, we encouraged you to take time for fun, for exploring, and for creating, and above all, to take time for laughter. Be certain you continue with that practice also.

Please take a few moments now to fill out your Self-Care Contract. Place it where you will be able to review it daily. You will notice that your self-care list becomes longer as you grow stronger.

In the early stages of grief, just getting out of bed or brushing your teeth may have been all the self-care you were able to achieve. By this time, you will have your acknowledgment box, a time to honor all you are and all you have done, and a time to list all that you are grateful for. Tier IV will show you how to step into your vision and complete your new goals one by one. By the time you complete this Tier, you will have learned how to schedule time to laugh and to have fun again.

Push yourself a small amount as you complete your Contract. Remember, we are here. We are your number one cheerleaders!

SELF—CARE CONTRACT

I, _____, commit myself to the following self-care begin-ning this week.

(List what you will actually do.)

(Make sure this is a realistic and measurable plan.)

I will begin working on self-care _____ for _____.

Date_____

Length of Time_____

When I achieve this goal, I will award myself with_____

_____.

I will evaluate the achievement of this goal with my support person. (Be certain to find someone to hold you accountable for this contract.)

Signed: _____

Support: _____

Date: _____

Exercises for Session 1

1. Continue to use a special place for doing your "inner work"—a place where you can listen to or read uplifting words. Be sure it is a place you enjoy being in, and that gives you a sense of pride and fulfillment. This place could be a separate room, a corner in a closet, or a special chair that you feel safe in and bless with your thoughts. This is a sacred place; treasure it.

2. Take five minutes daily to be in this special place, and say the words, "Today I will remember to honor myself at the deepest level. Today I will remember I am not alone. Today I will find a way to laugh and to have fun."

3. In Tier 4, we ask that you make a giveaway list. This will be an ongoing list of items you may want to give away now or in the future. All you will have to do is just begin the list. We will not ask you to give anything away that you are not ready to release. We would like you to step into a New Reality that you orchestrate, and as you live daily in that new place, notice what you can give to others. Your list might include old clothes, furniture, paintings, or photos. You might also consider giving away any non-productive thoughts and feelings. This list will also go in a place where you can add to it as new ideas surface.

   Do not judge this list. It is only for you, and you may write whatever you want. Remember, you do not need to act on the giveaway list; you only need to create it.

Weather Report Chart

Month/Year

Sun	Mon	Tues	Wed	Thu	Fri	Sat

TIERS OF HEALING IV
SESSION 2
YOUR NEW SCRIPT

It's when we are given a choice that we sit with the gods and design ourselves.
~ Dorothy Gilman
Every spirit builds itself a house, and beyond its house, a world, and beyond its
world, a heaven. Know then that world exists for you.
~ Ralph Waldo Emerson
By God when you see yourself, you'll be the idol of yourself.
~ Rumi

Song: "Hey Jude" by John Lennon and Paul McCartney

In this session, you will be writing a new script for your life. Imagine that your life is a movie and you are projecting it onto a screen. If you were to become the director of your life, what kind of script would you write for it? Think for a moment about your favorite movie. What kind of movie would you say your life has been to this point? For example, would you say it has been a tragedy, a comedy, a drama, a thriller, or a horror film?

Now take a moment to envision what kind of movie you would like to have your life portray in the future.

Think about the kind of person that you would like to be. What kind of qualities do you want to include in you, the main character of your script? What kind of clothes would you wear? How would you walk, how would you talk, would you wear makeup, and what type of hairdo would you have? Would you be healthy and fit? What kinds of foods would you eat?

In the area of spirituality, what do you believe? Are you searching for new meaning in your life? Are you content with where you are in your spiritual growth?

What family members and friends do you see in your new screenplay? How often do you see one another? What types of activities do you engage in together? What do your conversations involve? In what places do you gather for food, fun, and conversation?

As this picture of you takes shape, think about the community you live in. You may add things such as your home, your furniture, your garden, or your yard. Where is your home located? On what kind of street do you live? Are you in the mountains, near a lake, in the desert, or on flat land? What kind of car do you drive? Is it a jeep, an SUV, a convertible, or a truck? What color is it? This is your script; use your imagination to fill in all the details.

As we move on, think about your social life. What new activities are you engaging in? Are you taking classes in anything? Is there something new you have always wanted to learn? Where are you going to socialize? Who are you socializing with?

What do your finances look like? Do you have a savings account, investments, or a budget?

Now explore your career; what are you doing? What excites you about where you work? Where are you working?

Take a few moments to think of anything else you might want to add to this new screenplay of your life.

It is possible and actually fun to examine one's life as if it is a movie on a screen. Our beliefs, thoughts, and actions create the movies of our lives. Our interactions with others affect the scripts we write as well. It is up to us to determine what our lives will look like. It is our responsibility to look at the choices we have made in the past, and to evaluate what has worked and what has not. We have the freedom to choose the life we want. This may sound trite given the circumstances that have led us to this point in our lives; however, we have done enough work by now to know that we are responsible for the choices we have made in the past. Likewise, we are responsible for the choices we will make in this moment and in the future.

Your thoughts may be screaming that this is all fantasy. How is it possible to write a new script in a place of loss and futility? How is it possible to imagine a new life when what you really want is your old life? The facts may be hurtful; what you lost is gone. Remember the lessons in Tier 2 on acceptance. We do not ask that you act on what may be in your new script; we only ask that you begin the process of allowing yourself to imagine what type of movie you would like to write for your life.

Please get some paper and pen and review the above questions. Allow yourself to dream and imagine. You are never too old, never too young, and never too hurt to allow yourself the gift of imagination.

If you find that you are truly too upset to do this exercise, and you are in a place of being unable to imagine what type of movie you would like to star in, we urge you to get additional help. This course will never take the place of a professional counselor, as *it is not intended* for that purpose. You may check at www.tiersofhealing for additional resources, or you may contact your local mental health agency.

Exercises for Session 2

1. Think of the life you have been living as a movie. Give that movie a name and write it down. Here are a few examples: *The Night of You're the Living Dead*, *Fear Takes Over*, *The Big Easy*, or *Terror in Transylvania*. Use your imagination to discover a truly applicable name for the old movie script of your life.

2. Now, using the answers to the questions from this session, create a name for your new script. Here are a few examples: *Superman*, *The Ten Commandments*, or *An Angel in My Pocket*. This is your movie, and you may use whatever name you want.

3. Get a piece of poster board, markers, photos, glitter, and anything else you can find to make a movie poster starring you. Take your time and use care.

4. Once complete, hang your movie poster in a place where you will be able to see it daily for the remainder of this Tier.

To be nobody—but yourself in a world which is doing its best, night and day, to make you everybody else—means to fight the hardest battle which any human being can fight, and never stop fighting.
~ E. E. Cummings

Song: "The Impossible Dream," music by Mitch Leigh, lyrics by Joe Darion

In the NIV Bible translation it is written, "Then you will know the truth, and the truth will set you free" (John 8:32).

What do those words mean? What if we do not believe what is written in the Bible? What can we possibly hope to gather from those words? What if we have lived believing other people's lies and our own lies, and it has worked, or at least it has worked up to this point in our lives? What do these words mean, and are they helpful in our world today?

Then there is the question of integrity. Is it something to aspire to, and to demand in others and ourselves? What is integrity?

Here is what it states at www.dictionary.com
n·teg·ri·ty
[in-**teg**-ri-tee]
noun

1. adherence to moral and ethical principles; soundness of moral character; honesty.
2. the state of being whole, entire, or undiminished: *to preserve the integrity of the empire.*
3. a <u>sound</u>, unimpaired, or perfect condition: *the integrity of a ship's hull.*

Integrity means living in a place of wholeness. Our outward actions match our thoughts, feelings, and motivations—our inner world. We walk our talk.

We take our first step toward integrity by examining our inner lies. What do you tell yourself that is actually not true? Perhaps it is, "I will never be happy," or, "I will always be alone," or, "I am too old to start again," or our favorite, "I cannot do it."

Once you know what you are lying to yourself about, you may choose to hold on to that belief and the value you place on those words, but it will be impossible for you to truly believe what you tell yourself. At some level, you will realize you are lying. For example, let's look at our favorite: "I cannot do it." (I call this our favorite because most of us say it all too frequently.) The truth, however, is that of course I can do *it,* whatever *it* is. I may need to ask for help, take a class, spend additional money, or hire a trainer, but I *can do it.* Instead of saying "I can't do it," the honest statement would be, "I don't want to do it," or, "I do not want to spend the time, energy, or money involved to do it," or, "It is not important enough." Now I can see myself as powerful, no longer weak, and in charge of my own choices. That, in our opinion, is freedom.

The formula is simple: Find the lie, correct the lie, find freedom.

The problem is that most of us have no idea we are lying, and secondly, more than anything we want to be right. Our desire to be right is so strong that we would rather be right than happy. How do you find out you are lying? How do you accept you are lying and admit you are wrong?

When we lie to ourselves and to others, we are stepping outside of the parameters of integrity within our spirit and our souls. We harm ourselves. We may end up feeling guilty, ashamed, or self-righteous. All these emotions disempower us and leave us feeling small.

How often do you hear yourself using the words someday, maybe, should, might, but, or if? How do you tell yourself it doesn't matter when it does? What are you telling yourself when you don't keep promises to yourself? What do you say to yourself when you lie to yourself by ignoring, pretending, or denying?

To remember what DENIAL does to you on the inside, think of it as an acronym for **D**on't **E**ven **K**now **I** **A**m **L**ying. Often we are unaware that we are lying to ourselves. We do not stop long enough to be aware of our words, our actions, or the effects they will have on us. Lying to ourselves promotes self-sabotaging behaviors that keep us from having all we say we want in our lives. Our friend Debbie Ford once said, "The guilty seek punishment." When we are not true to others or ourselves, we set up a type of inner prison wherein we can only go so far before the bars of deceit stop us. Again, this happens at a subliminal level; we are barely aware that we are doing this to ourselves.

Your "get out of jail free" card involves taking the time to discover what is true in your life. In addition, it involves correcting the past and keeping your word now and in the future. You will need, you guessed it, paper and pen.

Exercise for Session 3

This may take more than a few minutes, and you may decide to devote a week to complete this exercise. Please let us know if you need our help.

Begin by turning a sheet of paper horizontally and making four columns. In the first column, you will write down all the things you tell yourself are out of reach and are therefore impossible to hope for or attain, and/or that you are convinced you cannot do, have, or be.

In column two, you will list the reasons you believe these things are true. For example, you may want to be the next quarterback for the Chicago Bears, and the reasons you cannot do this are because you are sixty years old, you were cut from your high school football team, and you are blind in one eye.

The heading of the third column will be "Is this true?" In the case of you wanting to be a quarterback for the Bears, the answer would be *yes*, because it is true that you cannot attain that goal.

The fourth column is where you can write options of things you *can* do to achieve each goal. In the scenario about quarterbacking, you could write, *Coach kids on throwing the football*, or *Join an adult touch football league*. You could also put this thought on the giveaway list.

As you work on this list, notice those areas where you have wanted to do or be or have something for a very long time and still do not have it. Examples may be an interesting job, a committed relationship, money in savings, and friends to play with. As you fill in column two, allow yourself to wonder if this reason could be some hidden belief you have that prevents you from what you say you desire. (Read more about shadow beliefs in *The Secret of the Shadow* by Debbie Ford.) As we compiled these lists, we realized that parents, teachers, and sometimes our culture had given us messages we believed as truths. Some of the most common ones were men are scary, money only comes to the greedy, be wary of other women because they will steal your man, you sing too loud, don't be a show-off, and money will not buy you happiness.

Once you discover other people's words running through your brain, you will be better able to decide whether they were telling the truth when they said those things, and whether that truth still holds up. Pretend for a moment that you are an attorney trying to prove the witness wrong. Let it be a game where the goal is to find the lie. It may have been true for others; it may have been true in the past; but today, right now, it is no longer true.

Once you find the lie, you can fill in your options in the fourth to-do column. Based on what you believe and say that is true, you can describe how to take action on that truth. Notice the feelings of freedom you have as you confront the lie and then step into a place of truth.

Correcting the past and making amends for past hurts is sometimes very difficult. For example, maybe you had an affair and no one knows about it; no one ever found out, yet you still feel the guilt. Rarely does it help to go back and confess. You will only cause more hurt and pain for everyone. If confession seems like the only way to find release from the guilt, find a minister or priest or rabbi and schedule some time with them to confess and purge yourself of the guilt. Perhaps you may want to give anonymously to the individuals who have been hurt. Or, you could speak to young marrieds about remaining faithful, and you could teach them how to maintain monogamy. In cases of theft or direct wrongdoing, a letter with a check may be good, and perhaps you will forgive yourself. Allowing yourself time to make amends for past hurts is one of the most freeing practices you can take. You may want to put this practice on your Self-Care Contract and do it weekly. Even unintentional mistakes can hurt others and cause us guilt; thus, they need to be resolved.

Vow to examine your behaviors and actions daily, and give yourself permission to find all the places in your life where you are not walking in integrity. It is only when we admit our wrong that we can make it right.

Loving Myself
I believe the single most significant decision I can make on a
day-to-day, day-to-day basis is "to love myself."
It is more important than my past, my bankroll, my successes or
failure, fame or pain, what other people think of me, my circumstances, or my position.
Loving myself is that single thread that keeps me going and warms
my heart. It fuels my fire and raises my hope.
When I love myself, there are no barriers too high, no valley too deep,
no dream too big, no challenge too great for me.
~ Adapted from a poem by an unknown author

Song: "Masquerade" from *Phantom of the Opera* by Andrew Lloyd Weber

In the beautiful song "Masquerade," one of the lines contains the lyrics, "Hide your face so the world will never find you." What a sad, sad line. We are born; we live in hiding so that no one will find us, and then we die, with no one ever having truly known us. What a very sad statement.

Each of us wears masks. Wearing a mask is not a problem. Perhaps there are times when it may be necessary to put on a mask, yet it is in the forgetting we are wearing the mask and then not taking it off that we rob others and ourselves of discovery.

Who are you really? You are a man, a woman, a parent, a child, a friend, but *who* are you? Many of us had masks placed on us when we were quite small, and if we attempted to take those masks off, we were punished, shunned, or even ignored.

Maybe you were told that you were the "good girl," "the helper," "the tough strong one." Were you shown love only when you wore the mask others wanted you to wear? Did you feel accepted only when you were being strong and tough, and you were afraid to let anyone know on those days that you were afraid?

Masks are not the problem. Believing we are the mask is the lie, and as we saw in Session 3, lying to ourselves imprisons us. Most of us have worn a mask at one time or another. Donning a mask may or may not be a conscious effort on our part to help us interact with those around us. Some of us wear the mask of humor. We cover what we are really feeling by making jokes, laughing, and trying to find something funny in everything someone says or does.

The very idea and reality of a mask separates us from others and actually prevents us from the deep intimacy each of us needs and craves. We pretend to be the person we believe we must be in order for others to accept us, and we create a false intimacy as we relate to others and the masks they believe they must wear. There is no real connection between us, yet we tell ourselves we are connected. We are not connected; our masks are connected.

There are times when masks can serve a purpose. Twelve-step programs use the saying, "Fake it 'til you make it." This has helped millions of individuals go from the powerlessness of addiction to the hope and health of living clean. Yet even as they "fake it," twelve-step programs have sponsors that hear the truth, and meetings where the group members encourage one another and support the truth of the struggle to change and accept. Such honesty comes from everyone in the twelve-step community knowing that he or she is wearing a mask until it is no longer a mask.

There may be times when you must give a talk in front of a group of people, and the fear has set your knees to knocking and your voice to shaking. This is a great time to put on a mask of self-confidence and perhaps even call upon the mask of a great speaker such as Martin Luther King or Gandhi.

The mask of smiling when you are angry may sometimes help soothe hurt feelings and bring about a happy conclusion, but remember, it is still a mask, and you may want to share the real feelings of your anger with a trusted friend or family member.

We do not encourage you to give up your mask(s), but we do ask that you acknowledge you are wearing a mask. Once you can admit to wearing the masks of being all grown up and independent and needing no help, you may then take the mask off when it is appropriate and put it back on when the situation calls for it. The important issue is to remember that you are wearing a *mask*.

When we don our masks at Halloween, it is more difficult to see others, to notice all that surrounds us, and even to breathe. At the end of trick or treating, we must take the mask off.

Exercise for Session 4

1. Using a paper plate, crayons, markers, and other art supplies, make the mask you wear most frequently. You may make more than one.

2. Go through your day and hold the mask each time you find yourself hiding behind it. The first step is to become aware that you carry and wear this mask.

3. Get with a trusted friend and have a conversation while you hold the mask in place. Now lower the mask and tell your friend one thing about you that the mask hides. If you feel free to do so, you can post what you hide on the Tiers Blog at www.tiersofhealing.com

TIERS OF HEALING IV
SESSION 5
HALF EMPTY/HALF FULL

That all things are possible to him who believes; that they are less difficult to him who hopes; that they are still more easy to him who loves, and still more easy to him who perseveres in the practice of these three virtues.
~ Brother Lawrence

Song: "Don't Worry, Be Happy" by Bobby McFerrin

Have you heard of Dr. Masaru Emoto? Dr. Emoto experimented with frozen water and ice crystals. One glass of frozen water was exposed to soft, soothing, loving music, as well as to light and loving phrases, while the other glass of frozen water was exposed to darkness, loud negative music, and shouted obscenities. When the molecules of frozen water were examined after these episodes, it was discovered that the water molecules in the glass that had been surrounded in light, softness, and love were perfectly round. The water molecules in the glass that had been exposed to darkness, negativity, and obscenities were misshapen and deformed. Since our bodies are made of more than 70 percent water, you can imagine what happens to us physically when we are exposed to either of these same situations. Other scientists have disputed Dr. Emoto's findings, and some have called his experiments pseudo-science. Yet much of what Dr. Emoto writes about and photographs is worth looking at. You can learn more about him on the Internet or by watching the film, *What the Bleep Do We Know!?*, a documentary that discusses the possible spiritual connection between quantum physics and consciousness. Dr. Emoto has a formula that he suggests be used as a tool to help us navigate changes and face choices in life. He calls this formula GAG, an acronym for the following:

G—Give thanks
A—Ask for love
G—Gratitude

It may look simplistic, yet science has now proven that our attitudes have the ability to change our physical bodies. Happier people live longer. Individuals who have spiritual practices, a community of friends, and who see the world as a good place tend to be healthier. We encourage you to at least try GAG.

Give thanks for what there is today.
Ask that love surround you and all that is.
Give gratitude for is the blessings in your life.

Is there ever a good reason to look for what is wrong and not look for what is right? Yes. Comptrollers and auditors must have this special skill. As you take inventory of your life, it is important to include all that does not work in addition to all that is good just the way it is.

As you look at your life and work with the question of the glass half-full or half-empty, remember this is a matter of balance. Has looking for what is wrong kept you out of shady dealings and away from a dangerous place, or has it kept you isolated and depressed?

Do you have the tendency to always look at what is right? Has that kept you in a dead-end relationship that could have ended years ago, or have you maintained a friendship with someone who borrows money, sucks your energy, and is only available when you are wearing your "everything is great" mask? Or, has looking at what is right moved you closer to joy, helped you laugh at circumstances, and made you the person everyone wants to be with? It is important to use both of these traits as you navigate the New Reality of your life.

Exercise Session 5

Take some time to ponder the answers to these questions before you write them down.

1. Where do you look for what's wrong in your life?

2. What do you see as negatives in your life?

3. What do you see as positives in your life?

4. How much time and energy do you spend thinking about the negatives?

5. How much time and energy do you spend thinking about the positives?

Notice whether you spend more time with the half-empty side of life. If so, find a way to be grateful for five things every day. Write these down. Also, as you encounter negatives in your life, ask yourself immediately what is right about the situation or the occurrence. This takes practice, but it is a habit worth cultivating. We are here to help you. We have been where you are. Contact us for help. anne@ tiersofhealing.com

If you notice that your life is spent in the half-full arena, congratulate yourself for being able to assess your life with honesty and clarity. Then, make a list of how the "glass half-empty" mindset has hurt you or how it has cost you physically, emotionally, or financially. Continue to be honest with yourself. At the end of each day, ask yourself if you could have said no more often, researched ideas more thoroughly, or taken fewer risks.

TIERS OF HEALING IV
SESSION 6
RELATIONSHIP PRIORITIES

Love is not primarily a relationship to a specific person; it is an attitude, an orientation of character which determines the relatedness of a person to the world as a whole, not toward one "object" of love.... If I truly love one person, I love all persons, I love the world, I love life. If I can say to somebody else, "I love you," I must be able to say, "I love in you everybody, I love through you the world, I love in you also myself.
~ Erich Fromm

Song: "Respectfully Yours" by Danny Stephens

As you set up your New Reality, it is vitally important that you review the priorities you have for relationships. Each of us has relationships with friends, family members, co-workers, bosses, spouses, ex-spouses, children, and all the people we meet on a regular basis. The world we live in is comprised of relationships. Even if you live and work alone, you have a relationship with yourself.

What is the number one priority in any of the relationships you have now or will have in the future?

Let's delve into the vast ocean of human qualities. We will begin by looking at the qualities we bring to a relationship, and then we will consider the qualities of others. Again, this is a great place to practice being in integrity with yourself and others, and telling the truth. You want to be sure that you or another really have the qualities you are identifying. You also want to be sure that the qualities you are seeking in a friend, partner, or boss really matter to you. What can you live with? What can you live without? What can you *not* live with?

It is a good idea to identify those qualities that you would honestly be willing to live with.

Let's look at some of the qualities you might like to have in a partner, a friend, or a boss. Make a list of ten qualities and character traits that you value, and that matter to you in a relationship. You do not need to rank your values; just make a list of ten values that are important to you. Then, in the interest of integrity, determine whether you are living these values. For example, most people who do a values list will put health and family in the top ten. When we ask them how many hours they spend with their families each day, many report twenty to thirty minutes, and some people have no contact with their family except on holidays. We spend time and energy on that which we value. Health is another value that we believe we have, but then we sit in front of the TV instead of taking a walk, we order the fries and not the veggies, we have not been to a doctor for a physical checkup in over five years, and we have no idea what BMI stands for, let alone what ours is.

Once you have made an honest list of your top ten values, you can then make a list of the values you would like to have in a friend or a partner or boss. If you have had relationships that have not been successful, it is vital and almost mandatory to write down the top values and behaviors you want in your next relationship. Your habits may draw you to the same type of person you have fallen for in the past. To avoid this trap, ask yourself, "Does this person value maintaining good health? Does this person value compassion? Does this person value fidelity and loyalty?" If the person you are dating does *not* have the values you are looking for, you *must stop* dating him or her, and then you need to reevaluate your wants. Do not think the person's values will shift, and do not kid yourself that their lack of values (that are important to you) does not matter. Values are what we live by; when we live in opposition to our values, we will not experience life at its best but rather life at its worst.

What kind of values do you need in a boss? Does your employer support the values you live by? If not, look elsewhere for a more satisfying job. Even in times of economic downturn, you can still look for a different place to work. If this becomes impossible, keep your values with you as you enter your workplace every day. This may seem difficult, but it is easier than living in direct opposition to that which you believe is important.

It can be difficult to stay true to yourself when faced with the possibility of financial gain if you turn your back on your top ten values. When our values are incongruent with what we do and what we believe, we will find ways to sabotage ourselves. We do not do this on a conscious level; rather, we unconsciously set up situations in which we are doomed to fail, become ill, or be fired.

Live a conscious life; know when you are in alignment with your values and when you are out of alignment.

Wheel alignment is necessary when it comes to maintaining a vehicle for safety. When you drive a car that is out of alignment, not only is it difficult to steer; it is a hazard to the driver, the passengers, and others on the road. This is true of our lives: We need to stay in alignment with our values.

Exercise for Session 6

1. Create your values list and keep it current. Our values change over the years. We update ours yearly and after any significant changes in our lives.
2. Use your accountability partner to keep you honest as you engage in new relationships or embark on new careers.
3. Ask those closest to you to share their top ten values. Ask what inspired them to list those particular qualities and character traits.

TIERS OF HEALING IV
SESSION 7
SPIRITUAL PRIORITIES

Some people talk about finding God—as if He could get lost.
~ Anonymous
At the beginning of the spiritual path, we are like children whose only real knowledge of themselves is a reflection cast in a mirror.
~ taken from the book Chop Wood, Carry Water by Rick Fields, with Peggy Taylor, Rex Weyle, and Rick Ingrasci, editors of New Age Journal

Song: "Gifts of the Goddess" by Karen Drucker

This session is about God, which is simply the name we give to a power that defies definition. Wars have been fought, people burned at the stake, and families torn apart because of this word, God, and all that it represents.

You may not believe in God or you may have a very different approach to what you may read in this session. You may even become angry and dismiss all of what you have done that has led to this point in your life because of what you will read in these few pages. We hope you will like what we write, but we know we cannot guarantee an outcome, and nothing sparks heated arguments more than the questions of who and what God is, but especially the question, "Is God real?"

We believe there is a God. We believe there is one Unifying Spirit—one Unifying Source that is beyond comprehension yet is totally within reach of our human experience. You may call this force The Universe or Buddha or Jesus. You may be an avid atheist, yet we doubt you would have gotten to this point in *The Tiers of Healing Self Guide* if you were because this is a spiritual process. Healing from loss is not the same as healing from the flu. If we could give you a pill and then tell you to drink plenty of fluids and call us in the morning, this course would have been much shorter. Healing, as with life in general, is a process, and it is a process of the spirit and with the Spirit.

Do you live by faith or fear? It is one of the questions in Debbie Ford's excellent book, *The Right Questions*. When we live by fear, we shrink; we hide; we are petrified. When we live by faith, we grow; we expand; we share. As with everything in life, the choice is up to you and only you.

Spirituality is not religion. Religion with its rules, traditions, and hierarchy is a left-brain experience. The left side of the brain is designed to get information from outside of us, and then to process that information and use it. Spirituality is a right-brain experience. Our right brain connects us with the essence of who we truly are. It involves our senses and the very rhythm of the planet, and it captures the whole picture of life, unlike the left side of the brain, which focuses on details and minutia.

Some of us love religion because we adore traditions, rituals, and the richness of generations worshipping the unknown and unseen. Others are absolutely opposed to organized religion and see it as a way and means of control and power. We are not here to convince you of anything. We ask that you allow the experience of the Spirit and your spirit to connect. In that place, you will know you are not alone.

You will know that life is magical, mysterious, and good. You will know God for whom you experience God to be.

How does a person find God? That is a question much like, "How does a fish find water?" God is all around. She is in the face of your beloved. He is in the face of your child. His power is felt in the wind and is seen in the lightning. Her gentleness is experienced in the warmth of the sun and the cry of the loon. You cannot escape God. You have the choice to turn away from the Spirit and deny it, yet as you do, you are in fact turning from yourself and denying your own divinity.

More has been written about the Spirit than any other topic, books and books and books: scholarly books, huge volumes of instructional books, metaphysical books, and witty down-home books. Spirituality is much like swimming or riding a bike. You can read about it for years, but it is not until you experience riding a bike or swimming in the water that you know what it is to ride or swim.

What is one way to connect with the Spirit? Be quiet. Sit still. Be still. Breathe. Listen. Ask. Be quiet. Sit still. Breathe. Listen. Ask. Continue this daily, two or three times a day for about five to ten minutes each day. It will take you a few (or many) days to be quiet and still. We have found the very early hours of the morning can be some of the best in which to do this practice. Prior to becoming quiet, imagine you are encapsulated in a beautiful bubble of pure light; suggest to yourself that only positive, uplifting energy will reach you. If your thoughts are loud and demanding, just breathe deeply and send your thoughts positive energy. They are only there because they were called. You need do nothing with them. Just breathe.

Ask for God/the Spirit to give you a sign, a feeling, and a sense of what is possible.

If you are having trouble quieting your mind, you might consider using some form of guided meditations. Sometimes it helps to have another voice guide you in quieting and stilling your own. Check out www.tiersofhealing.com for meditations and resources.

Meditation has become so popular that you can find several classes offered in almost every town in the United States today. Look in your town for classes on meditation. The Unity Church is global, and they typically offer classes and experiences in connecting to the Spirit. As it is written in Matthew 7:7 in the Bible, "Ask and it will be given to you; seek and you will find; knock and the door will be opened to you." Start seeking, start asking, and you will find what you need.

Please let us know if you require additional help, and let us know when you have connected. anne@ tiersofhealing.com

Exercise for Session 7

Write a letter to God/the Spirit with all your questions, including your anger (if any) and your praises. Ask for anything you may need now. Pay attention to what unfolds in your life. God works in strange ways, and the answers that come are not always the ones we expect.

You may put the letter in your acknowledgment box, put it inside a sacred book, or email it to us.

TIERS OF HEALING IV
SESSION 8
GIVING BACK

Use the talents you possess, for the woods would be very silent if
no birds sang except the best.
~ Henry Van Dyke

Song: "The Chain of Love" by Rory Lee Feek and Jonnie Barnett

You have reached Tier IV, Session 8. Congratulations! You have done so very much and are beginning to live your New Reality. How are you feeling? Are you having fun? Are you honoring yourself? Are you caring for your body, mind, and spirit?

You have moved through your pain and you have grown. Who are you now? What new gifts do you bring to this New Reality? What old gifts are waiting and wanting to be expressed in you today? When was the last time you took an assessment of the gifts in your life now?

There are many avenues for discovering your unique gifts. Are you interested in discovering your spiritual gifts, or do you want to discover how your talents and abilities can be applied in the workplace? What about the type of person you have become?

As a way to make these discoveries, we suggest doing an Internet search using your talents as keywords. Many assessments are free or cost very little and may be taken on line. Another excellent place to discover your gifts and talents is at your local community college. Contact the admissions office and ask about taking a test to discover your particular gifts. Knowing who you are and what you have to contribute will empower you to move forward in your life.

Once you have discovered what gifts you possess, decide what it is you truly enjoy doing. What did you want to do when you were eleven or twelve years of age? Those dreams do not leave us. The dream may need to be modified, but now is the time to allow it to grow.

Did you want to be a teacher? Is it possible to go back to school and get a teaching certificate, or would you prefer to volunteer as a teacher's aide or for your local literacy program? The Rotarians are a global group that raise money to assist their communities and the world. They have a keen love of literacy, and they would welcome a volunteer for one of their projects.

Do you love to dance? Volunteer at a retirement center, put on some music, and get the residents to dance even in their wheel chairs. Are you a born talker? Offer to serve on the hospitality committee at your local church. You are needed somewhere by someone. All you have to do is find your niche.

"I don't have enough time!" We hear this from the groups we lead. Anyone can find one hour a month to give back, to help, and to use what they know and what they love to help others. If you have more money than time, buy food and take it to the food pantry. You will feel the direct, positive impact of how your money is being used to feed hungry families. Be a part of your community. Become a Big Sister or a Big Brother. When you go to sporting events, or shopping, or jogging, take someone with you.

Do you want to change careers? Utilize your gifts to assure your happiness. Remember to match your values to your chosen profession. Changes do not need to be huge. You can begin slowly. Do you like to bake? Bake at home and find a local store that will carry what you produce. Check with your local state and county laws to be in compliance. Many large and successful companies started as small garage or kitchen-based businesses.

This is your life. You can choose to live your life or observe your life. What do you want to do?

Exercise for Session 8

1. Allow yourself time to explore your gifts, talents. and interests.
2. Read *Do It! Let's Get Off Our Buts* by Peter McWilliams.
3. Do the exercises in Mr. McWilliams's excellent book.

TIERS OF HEALING IV
SESSION 9
WRITE YOUR ROLE

If the heart wanders or is distracted, bring it back to the point quite gently.... And even if you did nothing during the whole of your hour but bring your heart back, though it went away every time you brought it back, your hour would be very well employed.
~ St. Francis De Sale

A tree as great as a man's embrace springs from a small shoot; a terrace nine stories high begins with a pile of earth; a journey of a thousand miles starts under one's feet.
~ excerpt from The Tao Te Ching of Lao Tzu

Song: "Let out the Joy" by Peter Schroeder

In the book, *It's Your Movie*, (find on Amazon or at www.peterschroeder.com) the author invites you to write your own role. This is similar to our session on creating your own script but we now become more focused.

In the script or movie of your life, what is the role you want to play? Your New Reality asks that you shape yourself into the person you want to be—the person you were meant to be.

What role have you played thus far in your life? Maybe you have played a damsel in distress, a dutiful employee waiting for the ax, or the good wife waiting on her family. What has been your primary role? Have you liked this role?

Maybe you enjoyed the role you were playing until the loss you suffered took that role away. As much as you would like to return to the role you played, it has been changed forever by loss. When that loss is grieved, accepted, and a new vision is found, a new role will emerge. Though different, it may be just as rewarding as the old role.

Some roles were given to us by our families and communities. Were those roles what we wanted? Were they assigned to us based on what we excelled at? No matter; it was decided we would fulfill those roles based on the needs of the family. Many dysfunctional families assign roles and then freeze each person into the exact place needed to support the dysfunction. Melody Beattie writes about this in her many, many books.

Finding the role you once played becomes easier if you look at your life as a movie. What was the title of your old movie? As you review your notes from Session Two, imagine who you were playing. Continue imagining what unplayed role you would like to take on. Would you rather play a hero in your new script or a victim? How would a hero dress? How would she walk? What would he say to the people he worked with or for?

Take a moment and allow yourself to believe there is a way to create the person you long to be. Is it a person of gentleness and compassion, or a warrior who rights the wrong he sees? If you do not enjoy the new role you have created, let it go and ask your spirit which role is best for you. Also, turn to the Spirit and ask, "What role will do the most good for me and for the world?"

Do you have children? Have you assigned them roles? If so, take steps to unassign those roles today. Humans are not automobiles. Humans are changeable, adaptable, and expansive, and we are designed to grow. The person your child was yesterday is not the person she is today nor will be in the future. Each of us has the potential to be anything we nurture. Pay attention to what you are nurturing.

There is a lovely story about a wise Native American chief talking to his grandson. There are different versions of this story; this one was found on the Internet at www.firstpeople.us

> An old grandfather said to his grandson, who had come to him in anger at a friend who had done him an injustice, "Let me tell you a story. I too, at times, have felt a great hate for those who have taken so much, with no sorrow for what they do. But hate wears you down, and does not hurt your enemy. It is like taking poison and wishing your enemy would die. I have struggled with these feelings many times."
>
> He continued, "It is as if there are two wolves inside me. One is good and does no harm. He lives in harmony with all around him, and does not take offense when no offense was intended. He will only fight when it is right to do so, and in the right way.
>
> "But the other wolf—ah! He is full of anger. The littlest thing will set him into a fit of temper. He fights everyone, all the time, for no reason. He cannot think because his anger and hate are so great. It is helpless anger, for his anger will change nothing. Sometimes, it is hard to live with these two wolves inside me, for both of them try to dominate my spirit."
>
> The boy looked intently into his Grandfather's eyes and asked, "Which one wins, Grandfather?"
>
> The grandfather smiled and quietly said, "The one I feed."

Perhaps you have heard this lovely tale at some other time in your life. It bears repeating because it is truth. That which you nurture, that which you feed, that which you spend your time and attention on will grow and become strong. What are you feeding?

Look at the life you have now; what role have you nurtured, cared for, and fed? Has it dominated your life? Has it expanded your life, given you peace, fed your life force? If not, you may wish to take on a role that does more for you.

Some roles in life we love, and then one day we awaken and find that particular role suffocating. There is no need to abandon a role that you have liked, but you can create another role and expand your repertoire. For example, the role of being a parent is immensely satisfying for so many, yet the day arrives when how we parent, how we mother or father our children, changes entirely. College, marriage, or a job transfer can bring on this change. You are still a parent, but because your child no longer lives with you, he or she no longer needs daily parenting.

We see this very clearly during divorce. Our child now has two homes and two parents who are living separate lives, and quite often, there are stepparents involved. In blended families, the role of parent has changed and adaptability is called for. What can you do with the extra time available while your children are visiting their other family? What new role can you add to your life? How can you rewrite your old role?

At the start of this Tier, you were asked to write your own script starring you—a script you would be interested in producing. In this session, we ask that you write a compelling role for yourself in the script you have begun to produce.

Exercise for Session 9

1. Decide what role you would like to try on, and make it over the top. If you have been quiet and mousy thus far in your life, you might want to try on the role of being loud and obvious. (You do not need to keep this role.) If you have been the victim, try being the superhero; if you have been a lazy, take-it-easy couch potato type, try on a type A role. Think about the role you have been playing, and then just for one day, play the opposite role. Make notes as to how the person in this role would dress, wear her hair, talk, walk, what he would do for fun, and so on.

2. This exercise can be done alone, but if you have a trusted friend or family member, it can be a day of laughter and fun if you do it together. Go to a costume shop and look at the costumes. Which ones are you drawn to? If possible, try on a costume and get into the role it represents. Go to a thrift store and again, try on various outfits you put together based on your notes. How do you feel when you are dressed more flamboyantly versus in a suit and tie? If possible, buy these clothes and wear them for the day. You and your friend can have a day of pretending, much like you probably did when you were a child.

3. This step is optional. Host a party where each person is to dress in his or her alter ego. Mild-mannered Clark Kent comes as Superman, always proper Sue comes as sexy, gum-chewing bawdy Suzanne. Notice how much freedom is afforded to all when they come in costume and play a new role for the day.

TIERS OF HEALING IV
SESSION 10
MAKEOVER

Life will bring you pain all by itself. Your responsibility is to create more JOY today and every day.
~ Dr. Milton Erickson
If the only prayer you ever say in your whole life is thank you, that will suffice.
~ Meister Eckhart
Give thanks in all circumstances.
~ 1 Thessalonians 5:18

Song: "One Moment In Time" by Albert Hammond and John Bettis

Take a deep breath and allow yourself to hear the words, "Well done. Well done." You have written your own script, cleaned up your integrity, and noticed the masks you wear. You've taken notes and drawn pictures and possibly used a glue stick. You have realized that how you look at life is what life will be—half empty or half full—and you have become more aware of the foundational priorities in life, relationships, and spirituality. In this last session, you had fun exploring other roles you could write and star in. You have done a lot of work in Tier IV, and you are to be congratulated.

Journeys take courage. Journeys take perseverance and commitment. Journeys take an open curious mind, and journeys take time. We welcome you into the group of individuals who have dared to move through grief and arrive a bit battered and shaken but knowing much more about who they are. You are capable of more than you thought you were capable of, and again, we congratulate you and honor your time here on this planet we all share.

This session is about doing a makeover. The following definition is from www.dictionary.com:

make·o·ver
   [**meyk**-oh-ver]

noun

1. remodeling; renovation; restoration: *The old house needs a complete makeover.*
2. a thorough course of beauty and cosmetic treatments:
   Assistants spent four hours on the actress's makeover in preparation for the awards ceremony.

What in your New Reality needs to be made over? You have changed your inner world. Does your outer world match your inner world?

You have changed and shifted your relationships and claimed your spiritual connections. Do you need a space to be still, to connect to the Spirit? This can be a small corner of a room that is sacred to you, or it can be a beautiful meditation space filled with music, candles, and all that touches your heart. Is your home a welcoming place where you can invite your new friends over for coffee or a meal? Is your home inviting to you? Does it reflect the New Reality of your life?

What about your community involvement? How do you want to restructure that part of your life? Does it mean dropping a few activities or volunteering to head a project?

Could your body use a head-to-toe makeover that reflects the added zest in your life? Do you need to find a workout partner and walk your talk about health? Look in your pantry; does it reflect the new role, the new script in your life? If not, change it.

Allow yourself the congruency of your outer world reflecting the brilliant inner world you are shaping.

Do your finances need an overhaul? Get a book, take a class, take charge, and set a plan in motion to make realistic, responsible choices about where your money comes from and where it goes. This might involve making a budget. Many churches offer free or low-cost classes in money management. Offer to trade services with a friend who knows how to budget and who needs what you have to offer.

Vow to continue giving to others what you no longer need. Schedule giveaway days annually—or better yet, monthly. Throw out the thoughts, feelings, clothes, attitudes, and events that no longer fit the person who is emerging.

Life is a journey. If you have completed all four tiers of the Tiers of Healing series, you have journeyed a very long way. You will continue to journey for many, many years. May you have a long, happy, prosperous life. We have been honored that you have spent a part of that journey with us. Keep in touch.

Welcome to a New Reality. May you find continued joy in each day you live.

Blessings,

Anne

anne@tiersofhealing.com

Thank you for completing *Journey To A New Reality* Tier IV in the series of Self-Guided Workbooks from Tiers of Healing.

We know the courage it took, and continues to takes, to move through loss and begin living an entirely new normal. All of us who have made this journey salute and congratulate you on all you do every day to stay on the path. We are here for you.

We ask that, if you have been helped in any small way, you would spread the message. Loss is part of living and there is a world of hurting people who may not know how to take the first step in healing. Perhaps they know but could use a helping hand.

We continue to be here for you. Stay in touch.

There is hope.

Anne

anne@tiersofhealing.com